Moments

GK Limcangco

AOS Publishing, 2025

Copyright © 2025

GK Limcangco

ISBN: 978-1-998662-83-8

Cover Design: Meredith Lindsay

Visit AOS Publishing's website:
www.aospublishing.com

Acknowledgment:

Sending deep gratitude and love to all the souls who shared a moment or more with me, allowing for this collection of poetry, prose, and stories to come alive.

I would also like to thank the writers and poets who gave their gift of creativity to the collective. Without the inspiration that they cultivated within me, I wouldn't have had the patience and motivation to write this book. Particularly, I would like to thank Jessica Semaan whose poem in her book Child of the Moon heavily inspired the piece "Paradox".

I would be honoured if you, my dear reader, will be inspired by this collection. That will make you reflect on those moments in your life, so you can appreciate them all. May you build your own library of moments because in the end, all we'll ever have are our stories.

In Love and Light,
GK

Moments

It's never about finding everlasting love
But finding beauty in the moments—
The joy in their presence,
The pleasure in their embrace,
Even the pain in the heartbreak

It's never about holding on until the very end
But learning all the lessons in order to grow:
The comfort in the silence,
The calm in their absence,
Even the sadness in saying goodbye

It's never about not wanting to ever feel alone
But knowing why we need to connect with another—
The love that we give,
The affection that we receive,
Even the wounds that we heal

It is all those fleeting moments that we will treasure
All because they can change us forever

A Paradox

Fleeting moments stay in your heart forever.

Here and Now

Nothing else mattered in the here and now;
It was only you and me in this moment
We just knew it somehow

And all it took for this simple bliss
Was my head on your shoulder
And a forehead kiss

Greedy Eyes

I surely thought about this day a million times over when I was still pining over you: the day when I see you again. I don't recall the scenarios I'd created in my head many years ago, but this was not one of them, because something is missing. In those scenarios, I'd always had feelings for you. I still wanted you. Now, when I look at you, I feel absolutely nothing—not even a tiny bit of attraction. You, on the other hand, are greedy with your eyes. I feel your gaze going over every curve of my body. I feel your eyes following me as I walk away. I'd be lying if I said that I don't enjoy it. I want you to want me, not to take away the pain of the past, of that heartbreak that you caused me, but for this moment of knowing that things have changed. That I no longer want you, but want me, you still clearly do.

Moments to Find

I know why I stayed, year after year
Even with this void, I still stood here
It was your warmth during cold winter nights
The push you gave to help me reach new heights
It was the conversations that lit me up
When I had a bad day, you picked me up
The space you gave when I needed to be alone
The interest in my thoughts that you had shown
It was your hand that wiped my tears
It was your presence that calmed my fears
And these moments were my reason
To be beside you with the change of each season
But the void was screaming loudly
So I had to follow it blindly
Because I have other moments to find
I'm sorry for leaving you behind
This was the only way that I could further grow
To become that person that I have yet to know

The Walk of Shame

It was nine am on a Saturday when she stood waiting for the train. She was wearing a black dress from the previous night. Her red beaded necklace was missing from around her neck. She quickly checked her purse to see if everything was in order. She sighed. Everything seemed to be okay, except her head was throbbing, and there was this looming feeling of emptiness that was starting to build up.

They met last night at The Cambie, a dive bar with sticky floors that served pitchers of cheap beer. He flashed her a cute lopsided smile, which seemed to have worked well to his advantage. He was pretty attractive, in a boy-next-door kinda way, so they started chatting. He was giving her some Spanish lessons and buying her more drinks while they sat on a covered billiard table. That seemed to be the last sober memory she had of the night.

She felt soreness on her index finger, so she examined it. The fingernail started to turn pinkish purple as she tried to recall what had happened. They drunkenly stumbled out of the bar to look for a cab, then he pinned her against the wall of a building to kiss her eagerly, crushing her finger in the process. "*What a souvenir,*" she whispered to herself.

She also remembered scattered pleasurable moments of the night with him, and then he woke her up a few hours later to tell her he had to work early that morning. He was pleasant with her and told her to stay for a little bit, but he didn't give her his number. Like a light bulb moment, she immediately understood why there was that growing feeling of emptiness. It's not like she was into him or anything like that, but in her previous experiences, she usually received a phone number Not this time. Any chance of future meetups was shut down. He didn't give her the luxury of making a decision about whether or not she would want to contact him after. And that rejection hit her like a train.

She saw the train approaching the station, taking her away from her thoughts. The train door opened to usher her right in. As she put one foot in front of the other to go inside, she almost wanted to pause, because in that moment, she felt it deeply. She felt that walk of shame.

Pieces of Me

I wanted to find pieces of me
In these places that you've been;
Hoped to hear a tiny part of me
In the songs that you sing

I tried to catch a whiff of me
In the air that you breathe,
Scoured your bed for bits of me
All around and underneath

I followed your trail with care,
Tracked down clues you left behind;
Searched the little things you share
As an attempt to read your mind

But I saw nothing of me.
Walked away, changed direction
Not knowing you hid pieces of me
In your thoughts, wrapped in affection

No Escape

I could not escape you
In every moment I breathed, you were there
You lived not only in my head
But in the deepest recesses of my heart
You went to every cell of my brain and wrote your name
You flowed through the veins of my heart, over and over
again
If sorrow is sweet,
I would taste like candy
And if love is a prison,
You threw away the key

Filling the Void

She really didn't know what she was to you. You just seemed to reappear whenever you wanted to, so when she met this guy at his get-together, she said yes when he asked her to stay over. And when she left his place in the morning, she had a skip in her step and a thought in her head slowly forming. She really did have a good night without you, because she filled this void that was in the shape of you.

Vulnerability

I remember how you reeled me in many years ago:
It was your stunning good looks and the fondness that you'd shown me
Then life pushed us on our separate paths
But fate brought us back in each other's orbit once again
Clearly, time and distance have changed us both,
And during our moments of reconnection
You have revealed a part of yourself you've never shown me before
Your words reflected your introspection;
It must have taken strength on your part to dig,
To break down your thoughts and your feelings, sorting yourself out,
And communicate to me what you have figured out
Do you remember that time when we were in bed and you told me that I was beautiful?
I will not forget that
Because now I want to tell you the same
But this beauty isn't what I see with my eyes
It isn't your stunning good looks that define the sheer beauty that I've seen with my heart
It's the accountability that you have shown
The feelings that you have revealed
It's the beauty that I didn't know mattered so much to me
Until you'd shown me your vulnerability

Hope

They say hope is a beautiful thing, but I disagree. Hope keeps you stuck. It plants you in a moment until it slowly eats you up, torturing you with hallucinations of happiness. Hope is cold-blooded. It makes you sit and watch the endless sky until you turn old and grey, still waiting for your shooting star. Hope is a thief. It sucks your precious time and takes away potential moments of joy, not allowing you to be fully present. Hope won't let you live, because it is what you live for.

Sundogs

She was fidgeting in her seat as she watched the vast snowy plains come into full view. The pilot had just announced that in less than fifteen minutes, they would be landing in Whitehorse, Yukon. She was full of excitement. Seeing the northern lights had always been her dream ever since she saw the animated movie *Balto* back in 1995; and in 2009, the dream was finally coming into reality. She was flying solo, only her second time doing so. When she saw that Air North was having an accommodation-plus-flight package, the deal was too good to pass up. When none of her friends could join her, she decided to make this trip a solo adventure.

She couldn't stop peeking through the window as she felt the soft thud of the airplane wheels making contact with the gravel. The small plane finally did a full stop and she hurriedly unbuckled herself and picked up her pink carry-on luggage from the overhead bin. She expected a blast of freezing air to bite her cheeks as soon as the airplane door opened, but the air was pleasantly cold; she slowly took the steps down, taking in the airport view. The Whitehorse airport says a lot about the town: small concrete airport building, massive space with snow-capped mountains hovering by. She wheeled her luggage through the exit doors, and in no time, saw her ride to the hotel.

It was mid-afternoon when she arrived at the Best Western Inn. It had an old saloon feel, pretty much another addition to the whole gold rush aesthetic of the wild western downtown appeal. After she checked in, placed all her stuff down, and inspected her big, clean, slightly dated hotel room, she found herself hanging out in the lobby to use the desktop computer to constantly check the weather and the aurora borealis forecast. There are two major factors in seeing the northern lights: one is the weather, because clear skies are needed to see the light show, and the other one is the actual aurora forecast; that night had a strong forecast but looked cloudy. She was also looking around for interesting things to do, since she had a full day the next day but had zero plans. The receptionist told her about The Sky High Wilderness Ranch that offered dog sled adventures. This sounded like the perfect northern experience, so she called them and made arrangements for them to pick her up at the hotel the next day.

She walked around the small downtown area but it seemed almost like a ghost town. There were only a few people walking around, including a small group of teenage kids who seemed to be looking for trouble, so it felt eerie and unfriendly. She went back to the hotel and hung out in the lobby to use the desktop computer once again while she waited for her northern lights tour. She would get picked up at ten pm at the hotel lobby so she had a lot of time to have dinner, relax, and freshen up. The easiest option for dinner was at the hotel restaurant and bar, which served breakfast and classic pub fare. She ordered a plate of ribs with a baked potato and side salad, and took her time eating it. By nine-fifty pm, she was already waiting at the hotel lobby. Nine-fifty became ten-fifteen pm, and for some reason, she got a little worried. She never confirmed with the tour company that she had arrived, or perhaps she really was just excited, because she was pacing around, worried that they had forgotten her. By ten-forty-fivepm, a tall, slim, good-looking white guy wearing a burnt orange-coloured toque confidently strode in. His pleasant demeanor and big smile was a stark contrast to her mid-pace, frustrated, and worried look. He smiled at her wider and introduced himself as Stefan from the Aurora Tales tour company, and his presence immediately took all her worries away as he led her to the van.

He told her that there were other people that they were going to be picking up, so if she wanted, she could sit in the passenger seat. There was a feeling of comfort that took over quite quickly as they talked about their background: her, a Filipino living in Vancouver, and him, an Austrian living in Whitehorse. The conversation flowed so smoothly even in between hotel pick-ups where Stefan had to go to the hotel lobby. He answered the guests' questions politely but he would always go back to their conversation. He told her about driving all the way up to Alaska and all the interesting sights he had encountered along the way as he pointed to the coyote that happened to appear on the side of the dark snowy road. She complained to him about the downtown feeling like a ghost town, and he told her it was usually the case when it was a long weekend because everybody in town went further out into nature. She asked him why he chose to live in Whitehorse, and he answered her with a sparkle in his blue eyes: *"I just love it here"*.

His enthusiasm made her more interested, and he must have felt this, because that drive to the campsite felt like it was only the two of them, in their little bubble, only interested in each other. They heard whispers and conversations in the back of the van but the conversations between the two of them just kept on going. When they arrived at the campsite, there was a group with another guide, and he introduced himself as Christoph from Germany, who seemed a lot more serious than Stefan. Both Christoph and Stefan showed the guests around the campsite and ushered them in a heated teepee with a wood-burning heater that crackled and cast a soft light from the glowing embers within the teepee walls. It had benches for everyone to sit on and a full stock of hot drinks and snacks that were readily available for everyone to partake in for the rest of the night.

The campsite was away from light pollution so they'd have the endless night sky all around them. The weather was cold, around minus ten degrees, but the small talk with the other guests, sharing stories about where they were from and why they were there and of course Stefan's company, as well as the heat and the glow from the campfire, kept her warm and cozy. They were all staring at the night sky, waiting for the light show, but a huge cloud was blocking their view. Stefan constantly came around after doing his rounds to make sure everyone was good and they had what they needed. He told her more stories about life up north as she listened with the same kind of wide-eyed wonder while watching the night sky. She was fully taking in all the nature around her, and even without a spectacular light display, everything felt magical. She found herself standing beside Stefan, staring at the sky in silence. There was no need for small talk because the silence they shared only honoured that moment. That was the kind of moment that might lose its sparkle if she added some useless chatter. For her, the northern sky was enough, but his presence made it even better because feeling him standing beside her felt like a warm hug that made her feel fully present and absolutely content.

By three am, they were all starting to head back to their hotel, and she immediately followed Stefan to the van and sat in front with him. Christoph came by and spoke to Stefan in German, and eyed them suspiciously before saying goodbye. All of the people in the van were quiet on the drive back and she was sure the other guests were so ready to dive in and be snug under the warm blanket of their hotel bed. Stefan finally dropped off a friendly middle-aged couple, they exchanged goodbyes, and as soon as they shut the car door, she felt a buzz in the air that said that they were alone again. She noticed him driving a tad slower as he brought her back to her hotel. She was telling him how excited she was to go dog sledding the next day and that she hoped the northern lights display would be much better tomorrow night. He parked the van and she was still trying to find words to say to keep him there, not really wanting to say goodbye, and he was gazing softly at her with his bright blue eyes, not saying goodbye. They spent a minute or two just sitting and he told her that he had the day off on Sunday. She had told him previously that she was flying back to Vancouver mid-afternoon on Sunday. For someone who was raised in a conservative culture where women waited around to be courted, she wasn't sure what to do with the information he had given her. She had an idea what he wanted her to do with it, but she just didn't have the tools to act on it. So she told him she would see him tomorrow. They let their eyes linger a little bit more on each other's faces, maybe even longingly, before she reached for the car door handle.

Her hotel bed was warm and cozy, and she wondered how much warmer and cozier it would have been with Stefan in it as she buried her face in the pillow. It was a little hard to sleep because she kept on thinking about his soft gaze and their interesting conversations and how she enjoyed the time with him. Eventually, sleep won over, and when she woke up, the seven am sun was peeking through the curtains, and cursed herself for waking up so early. She would be picked up at ten-thirty for her dog mushing activity, so after her usual morning bathroom routine, she just went down to the hotel restaurant and ordered a pancake and bacon breakfast. Her ride was on time; the driver was a nice middle-aged white Canadian man who didn't ask many questions but told her apologetically that he had to pass by Save On Foods to get some supplies. All she knew about him so far was that he owned the ranch. She watched him walk towards the grocery store from the backseat of the car and concluded that the whole town seemed to know one another as he stopped and chatted with passersby. She wondered if Stefan knew everyone as well, considering how friendly he was. The ranch owner came back with two plastic bags in hand and laid them on the passenger seat, and he drove them to the ranch.

She immediately saw many makeshift kennels sprawled all over the white snowy ranchland as soon as she got down from the car. There were a few ranch workers feeding the dogs, and one of them approached her. She was a strong French woman wearing a pair of mirrored sunglasses, and she introduced herself as Claire. She told her she was going to be her guide and as soon as she finished feeding the dogs, they could get going. She thought of Stefan right away and wondered how many Europeans had moved to Whitehorse, since all her guides were from Europe. She asked Claire if she could walk around and the French woman told her with a smile that they had puppies, and pointed to the shed in case she wanted to see them. Of course she wanted to see the puppies, so she walked over and called them using her sweetest puppy voice, but there was something different about these dogs. The puppies were standoffish and didn't act like domesticated puppies; she walked over to the kennels and observed the other sled dogs. All of them seemed different, like these dogs weren't needy for affection and attention from humans, and their existence served a deeper purpose. Looking at the tracks some of the dogs created around their kennel, it was very apparent that these animals lived to run. These were working dogs, and she could immediately notice how different they were from the dogs kept at home.

Claire told her that she was going to start prepping their sleds so she stood back and curiously watched while her guide approached the dogs. The dogs were going crazy around Claire. They knew what was going on and they were all barking as if to tell her to choose them. The chosen ones were seven dogs. Claire gave three dogs to her and kept four, then briefed her on what she needed to do, giving her instructions about how to pull the reins to be able to communicate with her dogs. The basics were how to make them turn left and right and to go fast and to slow down, and of course, to stop. It seemed simple enough, so she followed her guide, and soon after, she was driving her own dog sled. Claire took her to this vast frozen lake where she felt the cold and very fresh northern air brushing her face as she sped up behind her guide. She was enjoying herself so much that she didn't think of Stefan at all. Claire slowed down and stopped in the middle of the frozen lake. She motioned for her to do the same, so she did, and told her that they could take photos. They indulged in a little bit of small talk while Claire took photos of her and the dog sled. She took the opportunity to take in the breathtakingly beautiful scenery. *"No wonder Stefan loves it here"*, was the quick thought that passed through her mind. She found out that Claire was actually French-Canadian and was only spending a few months in Whitehorse. Soon after handing back her trusty point-and-shoot camera, Claire took one dog from her own sled named Tweety and added this dog, so her three-dog sled became four.

Tweety was so full of energy that she was zooming past the forested area and failing to control her sled. The personalities of the dogs stood out as she instructed them to go. Her alpha dog was a black male dog called G-throw and his sidekick, the one running beside him, was an older white dog named Shirley. Rose, a younger brown dog placed in the back, looked a little bit unsure of herself as she kept on looking back at her, as if waiting for her to give her instructions. With Tweety in the mix, a young brown female dog that looked a lot like Rose but full of confidence and enthusiasm, she tumbled a few times. and all she could hear as she was getting up and brushing herself was Claire yelling, *"Control your dogs!"*. It took a while for her to get used to the extra boost, but as soon as they got to the frozen lake, she was speeding so fast that Claire had to make an effort to catch up just to tell her to stay behind her. The experience was so exhilarating and incredibly special that she was sad to say goodbye to the dogs, to Claire, and to the ranch, but knowing that she was going to see Stefan again made the goodbyes a little better.

She was driven back to her hotel just after one pm by another person named Greg with his dog called Tiny. He was a lot friendlier than the ranch owner and asked a lot of questions about the Philippines. She was looking forward to sitting down for a meal and hopefully nap because she was feeling tired. She saw some of the shops close to the hotel were open so she went into one that sold soaps and *au natural* body products, and bought herself bath bombs and massage oil. She went back to the saloon and got herself a pint and a delicious salmon barbecue burger. She felt a bit buzzed from the beer so she went back to her room, filled the tub with water, threw a bath bomb in, and bathed until relaxation crept in. She dove straight into bed wearing only her hotel bathrobe. She had one solid hour of sleep; the rest of the time, she was just tossing and turning in bed and going over the day, and of course thinking about Stefan. By sevenpm, she was out of bed and headed back to the restaurant, but it seemed very busy. They were setting up a drum kit and putting up mic stands so she figured they would have live music for the evening. She ordered fish and chips this time and felt a little bit uncomfortable as small groups of older white men with a redneck vibe started coming in. She didn't stay long at the restaurant and killed time in the lobby with the desktop computer. The internet had informed her that the Aurora forecast wouldn't be as strong as the night before but the sky would be clear.

By ten pm, she was tingling with excitement. She had one more chance to see the Aurora Borealis and to hang out with Stefan, so imagine her disappointment when stern

Christoph came in the lobby to look for her. He slid open the back door of the van, motioning for her to go inside. She followed and kept quiet all the way to the campsite as they picked up a few more guests and greeted them with a half-smile when they entered the van. When they got to the campsite, there seemed to be more people. Stefan was talking to an older man with a dog and a younger man in German when he saw her walk by. He greeted her with a big smile and she could have sworn he sensed her disappointment. The campsite seemed livelier than the night before, and she mostly chatted with a big Chinese-Canadian family from Vancouver that were welcoming and fun, and a quiet Asian couple in their twenties, most likely a new couple since the girl made her feel like she was invading their space.

Stefan was also busier, having a bigger crowd; sometimes she was fully by herself, so she would go further away from the teepee and the campfire. There was also a very annoying kid from the big family who kept on following her around asking her what grade she was in, because she looked familiar to him. She was thirty, and she knew she looked younger than her age, especially because she had a bob haircut with bangs, but it was another level to have a kid who was probably fourteen that kept trying to converse with her. There was also a very loud Mexican family that wouldn't stop singing. She gave them the stink eye, took out her iPod, and placed the earphones in her ear while walking past their group to let them know how loud they were, but some people just didn't care. She was really hoping Stefan would spend time with her like the night before, but the good thing about this place was that it was too stunning for anyone to feel disappointed or alone for more than a minute. She was standing a few feet away from the group, staring at the night sky. It was not a strong light show, but she clearly saw why they called it the dancing northern lights because it was moving so gracefully in the glorious endless night sky.

She felt Stefan's presence right beside her and told him she was happy to see how the Aurora Borealis dance, and he responded by asking her why she was quiet that night. He said he noticed that she wasn't talking much. She told him she was tired because she had a full day and told him about her dog sledding adventure and how much she enjoyed it. They continued to watch the sky in silence this time around, but just like the night before, she loved every bit of that moment with him beside her under the majestic northern sky. She wasn't even sure what made that moment truly memorable. Was it Stefan, Mother Nature, or both? She didn't get to hang out with Stefan the next day. He was giving her some tips about which places she could check out that were walking distance from the hotel and he mentioned again that Sunday was his day off and that he was probably not going to do anything. It felt like another nudge for her to ask him to hang out, and if it was, she just didn't have the courage to do it.

When they started to pack up, she knew her time was up. She said goodbye to Stefan and she wanted to at least hug him; she felt he wanted to as well, but because it was established that he was her guide, rather than a friend, it was a little awkward. The hesitation was palpable when they stood face-to-face, saying their goodbyes. She dragged herself as she followed Christoph back to the van and was greeted by loud drunken noises coming from the hotel restaurant and bar. She felt intimidated by the noise and rushed to her room, changed, and dove right into her bed. It was easy for her to fall asleep this time around so it was apparent that she was really tired. The next day, she took her time getting out of bed. After packing up, she checked out, and was going to sit down for a breakfast sandwich at the restaurant that now smelled like stale beer and man

22

sweat. Even the chairs and tables looked hungover, so she went out and found a hip and artsy cafe that served quality croissants and fancy smoothies. She was happy to sit and enjoy a nice breakfast, and she took her time with every bite because she had time to kill.

She walked around the small downtown again, but this time, it felt a lot more welcoming, and there seemed to be more life and activity. She went into a few more stores and got some interesting souvenirs for family and friends. Soon after, she walked to SS Klondike, a National Historical Site by the river. As she was walking and taking photos, she noticed how everything felt different there. The air felt different and the light; the light was extraordinary. She was admiring the reflection of the sunlight on the frozen glass of the streetlamp that seemed to create a halo of multi-coloured lights. She suddenly remembered Stefan telling her about sundogs. Sundogs were bright coloured areas of light beside the sun. When the light was refracted through the ice crystals, this phenomenon occurred, and it almost looked like a second sun. She smiled, thinking about Stefan, their time together, and how he made the northern sky even more magnificent. Sometimes, people do come into your life just to make a moment more special. She took another minute to observe the light. She could hear Stefan telling her how spectacular sundogs were, and right then and there, without any hesitation or doubt, she believed him with all her heart.

Beneath the Surface

Everyone thought you moved on
With this new girl in your arms
You made it look so easy
It even set off all my alarms
But when we got to talking
You told me a different story
How you still thought of me
And how you were sorry
That moment clearly showed me
That things are not what they seem
It may be different beneath the surface
Where the actual truth will be seen

All in the Kiss

It was in that moment, when their mouths were deeply locked onto one another's, feeling this intoxicating blend of passion and tenderness. It was right then when she remembered how absolutely delicious it was to kiss. She was surrendering to all her senses and allowing them to wake her up, only to find herself in a dream, a long-forgotten dream. Perhaps a dream long-forgotten because time, circumstance, and the wrong men had buried it deep. But now that she had awoken to this kiss, she vowed to never ever forget it again.

Pure Clarity

It all made sense to her
In this moment of pure clarity:
She needed him to heal
And he needed her to find himself
But now she had healed
And he had found himself,
So they said their goodbyes
To the new versions of each other
Because even if it was not written in the stars
That they will be together forever
They are still forever changed
By the presence of one another

Underneath the Wave

She felt her tears pool on her pillow. She didn't even bother wiping her cheeks—it was her way of surrendering to the wave of sadness that was hitting her quite hard. She wondered when the echoes of his words would finally stop dragging her under, taking her deeper and drowning her in this sea of torment. Definitely not today. As she felt another wave of sadness coming closer, she felt one more emotion underneath it all. Was it hope? Was it joy? It felt good despite all the tears. She welcomed that glimmer of feel-good with a sense of curiosity. She had been here before, but something was different. She quickly remembered the first time around. She thought that she would never feel intensely for someone else, ever, and yet she was here, brokenhearted again. That thought made her pause and have a moment of self-reflection. And from that came a breakthrough, a deep knowing that love could and would happen again. She hung onto that hope, to that joy underneath the wave of sadness, as she wiped her cheeks with the back of her hand, a smile on her lips.

Options

I was thinking of you all day, waiting for a message, hoping you'd have something to say. But all I heard was silence, and to be honest, I'm drowning in your absence. I took a breath to calm my anxious mind, at this point I'm feeling so resigned. But this was until I saw him from afar, walking towards me, looking like a star. He looked at me brightly, smiled, and then nodded politely. And at this moment I just knew, it really doesn't have to be you.

My Stubborn Heart

Forgive my stubborn heart
It will not listen to anyone who will take you apart
Even with the cold air you blow in my face
It will find warmth in your past embrace

Forgive my stubborn heart
Clearly, it isn't very smart
It will find hope in the tiniest crack
Forgetting you will feel like an attack

Forgive my stubborn heart
It always goes right back to the start
And even if you run far away
It will always find you, and beside you, it will stay

Happy Nostalgia

They were making small talk like they were strangers. It had been almost two decades since they last physically saw one another. They roughly knew of each other's lives through social media. Then on this day, fate made them randomly meet again, in her city, in her bikini, while she was laying on the beach with a friend.

He was talking about living in the Bay Area and telling her that he and his family were vacationing in Vancouver. She greeted his wife and kids behind him with a smile and then watched his mouth while he was speaking, still making sense of what was unfolding. It was like her teenage self was coming out of hiding to meet his teenage self, because when they said their goodbyes, he looked back at her and silently mouthed— "*what the fuck?*".

And in that brief moment, it felt like they were back in Manila, in college, when they were best friends until feelings made everything complicated. But now, none of that mattered, because she was basking in this happy nostalgia. When he mouthed those three words to her, all she could think was— "*now there's my best friend*".

Our Eyes Could Never Hide

I was in another's arms when I felt your gaze
I looked up and saw your face
From across the room we locked eyes
Stared at one another like a prize
In that moment, time and space didn't matter
Because we only had eyes for each other
No words needed to be spoken
This bond between us remained unbroken
Because our eyes could never hide
All these feelings that we both denied
But reality had to step in
Our egos wouldn't let us win
So we both looked away and acted fine
Even though our hearts were on the line

Reciprocity

"You get what you give" — says transactional love
"Love is free" — says unconditional love
"Love yourself first" — says self-love
"Find a good balance" — says emotional fulfillment

The Prey

I was bad at pretending
I pretended 'I don't remember' when he told me he loved me
I also pretended 'I don't remember' kissing him back, saying I was too intoxicated
But at that moment when you pretended that 'you don't remember me', I just knew
The wheels have turned
I have been the hunter before
But now, you have made me the prey

Breadcrumbs

You gave me breadcrumbs but I ate them like a feast
Made it a reason to say you wanted me at least
Waited eagerly, even patiently, at your table for more
Then you gave me a crumb, even tossed it on the floor
I felt confused because I didn't want to walk away
Then insulted that you thought that was all it took for me
to stay
Because you just scattered your crumbs to get something
So you really gave me nothing
And that was the moment I realized
Even turned to myself and apologized
I was teaching you that I deserve less
More so if I keep on giving you full access
I do like you but I like myself more
And if you want to come back again, knock on my door
Better bring more than your breadcrumbs to me
Show me that you know it's a privilege to have this chance
with me

Thank You

When I told you I had unconditional feelings for you, it didn't mean you had to love me too. A 'thank you' would have been nice, but an ice-cold rejection wasn't enough; you also allowed the potential destruction of my life to happen. But at that moment, when my last bit of anger had subsided, I realized that you don't see love the same way I do. You see it as ownership and possession, and give it conditionally, so how can you ever understand unconditional love when you can't even receive it freely? Even if you didn't thank me, I'm thanking you for making me understand. It's never just about giving love but also having that capacity to receive love. In a way, I feel sorry for you. Maybe one day you will understand it, and see yourself worthy to receive it.

Movie Moment

"One double Jack and coke, please," I told the bartender as I took a step up to get close to the wooden bar area. I felt a pair of eyes boring holes at the back of my head and when I twirled around with my drink to step down, I found out that those eyes belonged to this really good-looking man with deep blue eyes and brownish black hair. He was wearing black pants and a white button-down shirt with sleeves rolled up to his elbow, exposing his tattoos. He was standing there, staring at me with so little shame that when I looked up at him and walked past him, I still felt his eyes on me.

I knew who he was. His name was Jamie and he sang for one of the bands that we came here to see. His band played music that sounded a little bit like that British rock band Muse, which I wasn't crazy about but still enjoyed. This was not the first time I had seen Jamie sing on stage. My friend Erin who took me to this gig was good friends with this girl who went to high school with Jamie. The other band who Erin wanted to see, who she's friends with, was also friends with Jamie. I was pretty much in this familiar territory that night where everyone seemed to know one another, so it was only a matter of time when Carly, Erin's friend, came up to me and whispered, *"Jamie wants to meet you"* over the loud music. I looked up at her, not as surprised as I thought I would be, since I caught him staring me down. *"He has a fetish for small Asian girls.",* she added, clearly making a joke. A type of joke one makes when you have known a person for a very long time. In this case, Carly and Jamie have known one another since high school.

I honestly didn't think Jamie would give me the time of day. It's not like I think that I was not attractive enough for him.

There just seemed to be a lot of competition. I only saw his band play a couple of times and I would see him hanging around their band table close to the stage where women would be hovering around. From my point of view, it was apparent that he knew that he could easily take his pick. I mean, it is one thing when you play in a rock band, but you take it on another level if you have the looks, and he definitely had them. He could probably even pick two or three at the same time and I think these girls wouldn't even mind. When he approached me, though, he had none of that aura. He seemed generally interested to know me and my background, and was even excited when I told him that I was born and raised in the Philippines. He showed me his tattoo with alibata on it, and told me that his ex-girlfriend was half-Filipino and that he spent a few months in the Philippines.

The more we conversed, the more interesting he became. He was a year younger than me, an artist, and most importantly, we had similar musical taste. I told him that I would forever be a nineties music fan and he immediately asked me if I would like to come with him to see a local band that played only Radiohead. *"A Radiohead tribute band?"* I asked him, fighting with the music to be heard. *"They have those?"* I added as he nodded at me waiting for my answer. *"Sure, I'm up for it!"* I said enthusiastically.

I went to Lauren and Carly, who were mingling with their friends and acquaintances close to the bar. I told them that I was going to the Railway Club with Jamie and they both gave me a knowing look and told me to take care. The live music wasn't finished at this bar and the last band was still prepping on stage, but I already saw the bands that we came to see, Jamie already played his set, and there was better music at the other venue, so we both stepped out of the bar into the fresh summer air. The night wasn't very young, around one am young, but it felt like it was only getting started.

The venue that we were going to was only a twelve-minute walk to where we were. One thing I love about Vancouver is that the downtown area is safe and small enough for you to be able to walk around, whatever time it may be. I had enough alcohol in my system to be happily tipsy and most likely even tipsy babbling to Jamie, but he was paying attention and was even gently leading me by touching my lower back as we walked. When we reached the venue, Jamie talked to the bouncer, who he seemed to know very well, and gave us a stamp on our hands without asking us to pay for cover. There was a staircase leading up to the bar and a crowd already forming, waiting for the band to start. Jamie took my hand and led me right in front of the stage, squeezing through the crowd. He asked me what I wanted to drink and told him I have been drinking Jack and cokes, so I'd have another one of those. He disappeared into the crowd as the band started to play "Karma Police".

The band had every right to call themselves a "Radiohead tribute band" because they sounded like Radiohead without trying too hard. After the first song, I felt Jamie's chest touch my back, almost feeling like I had a wall of protection behind me as he leaned forward and stretched out his arm to give me my drink. I looked up at him with a smile to say thanks and he leaned in for the sake of being closer to me. The girl beside me kept shouting, *"Idioteque! Idioteque!"* and when I looked at her, she looked back at me and said with conviction, *"It is the greatest song ever made."* I gave her a thoughtful smile and nodded. I was obsessed with this song during my college days, and even if I won't consider it the greatest song ever made, it's a song I highly regarded. I thought to myself, " *Would they even play that song? And if they did, would they even do it justice?"*

Throughout the set, Jamie would lean in to check if I was having a good time, and I really was, so much so that I had to turn around to give him a hug during "High and Dry", which was pretty high on my favourite Radiohead song list. He looked down at me while I had my arms around his neck and he gave me a soft kiss on the lips, and I had to stop. One thing he didn't know was that I had a boyfriend. It was not a serious relationship but it was still something, so I turned around, and that was when they started to play "Idioteque". The girl beside me was going crazy with her friend, jumping around and loving every second as they played the song. It was indeed ear candy, surprisingly. I really didn't think that they would be able to pull this song off, but they did, and if life had a pause button, this would be one of those moments that I would revisit. The song, the bar, the band, Jamie. That moment.

When the band finished their set, we ended up on Granville Street, the entertainment district. The city closes the strip to vehicles, making it pedestrian only on Friday and Saturday nights, so you often see groups of intoxicated people stumbling out from a bar or a club, walking in the middle of the road most likely to get a slice of pizza or any street meat or fast food before they head home. I told Jamie that I had such a great time with him and that I really loved how he took me to see that band, but I also needed him to know that... *"I have a boyfriend,"* I told him. I did see disappointment in his deep blue eyes but it quickly turned to "it's all good" as he looked away and said that we can still be friends. I told him I would love that. He sat down on the sidewalk and I tried to do a sobriety check, trying to walk in a straight line by walking inside the thick yellow lines painted on the road. I was laughing and saying whatever would come out of my intoxicated mouth. When I turned to look at him, I saw him watching me intently. His gaze started from my gray boots, up to my legs, to my denim mini skirt, all the way to my black spaghetti-strap with a black-white-gray shoulder cover up, and smiled when he reached my face. I stood there and I took that all in, because honestly, it felt so good to be looked at that way if the one looking at you is also someone you could look at just the same. We eventually had to end the night and told him I could walk myself home. He wanted to get out of the strip so he could easily hail a cab, so he walked me halfway and we hugged and said our goodbyes.

A few days after I met Jamie, I found myself walking on Granville Street after work. On a regular day, Granville Street loses its magic to bums on the sidewalk and people and cars rushing to get where they need to go. Jamie had recently added me on social media, and I was still trying to make sense of it all. I found the spot where he was sitting and where I was walking in a straight line and I stopped for a second. I told myself that if I explored this, it might just blow up in my face, so there was a little bit of confusion, but I also had a nice realization. For many years, one of those movie moments that I have seen unfold onscreen and secretly wished to have happened to me was being out and randomly meeting this amazing guy and spending a great time with him, walking around the city until the wee hours of the morning. No sex involved, but intimate nonetheless, and it felt like this was one of those movie moments. Those moments that would bring a smile to your face when you sit and reminisce. It was one of those for me. Would it even matter what would happen next? When I go through snippets of memories like watching movie reels in my mind, this moment was perfect, so perfect, it even had Radiohead as a soundtrack.

Twinkle

She stopped him mid-kiss and whispered breathlessly, "*You're great*", letting her words linger as she searched his face. He paused to look at her, but didn't say anything. But in his moment of silence, his green eyes twinkled, just like dainty fireworks sparking up the night sky. He didn't need to tell her anything, that twinkle in his eyes said everything.

Pictures of You

I have pictures of you in my head
I framed them, hung them over my bed
Hoping to dream of you every night
Because in my dreams you hug me so tight

I looked at pictures of you on the internet
Reliving the time that we've met
Like little souvenirs that I've kept
Feelings underneath my bed that I've swept

I drew pictures of you to remember
Those precious moments we spent together
Because these pictures are all I have of you
Even if I drew them in the deepest shade of blue

A Promise of Ever After

The idea of happily ever after brought disappointments many times over. I don't think I'd want to make promises of forever; instead, I'll find contentment with moments spent together. And if we have to say goodbye to each other, I promise that I'll think of you fondly ever after.

Karma Continues

It was that moment when I heard the words that came roaring out of your mouth. I knew without a single doubt that you wanted to hurt me. Your words were thrown like grenades at my heart, maliciously and intentionally, as if to get back at me for all those years that I had ignored you. And I just sat there, letting you blow me up into pieces while you showed no remorse. When you were done, I had to gather up my bits and pieces from your car and you sent me home crying with my head down.

Circles

When do I change the ending of
This unfinished symphony of us?
Is it when I start understanding
How things transpired between us?

That exhausting loop I have been on
It kept me going around in circles
That even when you were long gone
I still jumped these internal hurdles

Then I saw this toxic consistency
The patterns I needed to break
A push to do things differently
And all the changes I had to make

Linger

I am a moment that will linger even if you try to bury me deeper. I will not only haunt you at night in your dreams, but also in your waking life with daydreams. You will regret the things you haven't told me yet, and deep inside, it will make you fret. It's because you thought you could easily forget me. Even time won't let you escape me, but the question is, will you face your fears and face me?

Schoolgirl Crush

"What happened to 'I absolutely want to see you again'?" she thought as she refreshed her email, hoping that a response from him would magically appear. She let out a big sigh. He knew all she wanted was a summer fling because she was leaving, so she didn't understand why he couldn't just have fun with her. She took a moment to assess herself. *"What is this I'm feeling?"* she asked herself curiously, becoming more aware of this mild pang in her heart that felt a little familiar. This was when she realized what it was. This was the feeling she had in high school when she heard that her crush liked someone else. This was infatuation pain. And even though it made her feel things that she didn't necessarily like, she came to terms that she actually missed it. She missed it, not in a masochistic kind of way, but more nostalgic, like coming back to a time of blissful innocence, when being giddy wasn't a rare occurrence. She suddenly realized that she had nearly forgotten what a schoolgirl crush feeling was like, so she allowed herself to feel, even swim in it, despite those ripples of discomfort. She smiled to herself as she refreshed her email once again.

Ashes

I thought my love for you would continue burning
Ever so slowly until the end of time
But it was all-consuming
It burned me down like a crime
Until there was nothing left of me
But my ashes and my love for you
Then something had risen from what was left of me
And it was all because of you
You walked away but my love still won
From my ashes, I bloomed like a flower
It birthed a new me that I never would have known
A phoenix with my newfound strength and power

A Warm Welcome

You didn't need to tell me you love me. I already knew. I felt it in that moment when you kissed me deeper, more earnestly than ever before. I was not sure if I felt the same way, but I welcomed it anyway.

Burn

I couldn't let you get that close to me
Because you always managed to burn me
After you showed me this potential between us
You held back, kept me at a distance

And these moments took a bit of strength
Just to keep you at arm's length
Because I couldn't stray too far away
That glimmer of potential was making stay

So when you burned me with coldness
I came back with this boldness
Trying to be a player in your game
Winning you over was what I'd claim

Until one day, I was done
Burned you with a cold one
Said goodbye, finally gave up
You lost me and you had to wake up

Last Goodbye

They clung on to each other just like a million times before. But tonight, tonight was different from all the others, because this would be their last. Their bodies sensed it, their hearts knew it, and because of that strong sense of knowing, nothing could get in between them. All their problems, all their frustrations, doubts, and insecurities, everything that haunted them both seemed to disappear. They were completely impenetrable. Because all that mattered was this moment that they had, of savouring one another for this very last time.

Version of You

She carried you in her heart for many years
Held you in a special place despite the tears
Because those brief moments of bliss
Even time wouldn't let her dismiss
Then one day you somehow reappeared
Gathered courage, said things she had feared
She spilled her heart out to a version of you
Only to find out that you were not the version she knew
She took off the rose-tinted glasses she wore
And to your new version she swore
Then she buried that version she knew
With all the moments she had spent with you

A Gift

She was sitting on a bench at David Pecaut Square on King Street West in downtown Toronto. She was looking up at the sky, letting the warm sunlight and the chilly spring breeze take turns kissing her cheeks. She felt absolutely content in that very moment that her lips weren't the only thing in her body that was smiling. Her whole being was smiling.

This feeling that she was experiencing was almost the same as opening a present and expecting something nice, but what you received exceeded your expectations. That was that feeling that was taking over, and she wanted to pause, savour the moment. Bask in the feel-good.

She was also killing a little bit of time sitting at a park across the Royal Alexandra Theatre, waiting for the Broadway musical *Dirty Dancing* to start. At the same time, she was also taking stock of what had already transpired during her first solo trip. She felt that seeing a show was a perfect way to cap off her five-day vacation in Toronto. Technically, it was a nine-day vacation if she added the four-day train ride from Vancouver to Toronto. Train rides always fascinated her. There was something about looking out at the fast-moving scenery outside the window. It seemed so introspective, like trying to make sense of life when you are sitting still, observing it while it passes you by. She also felt it was a great way to get to know her new home like a nice long handshake as they moved through each province— British Columbia, Alberta, Saskatchewan, Manitoba, and finally, Ontario.

The train ride was nice and peaceful, but was such a long journey, so when she got to Toronto, she was beyond excited to explore and socialize. She had friends to meet—a former coworker and her family, a college friend, and some grade school schoolmates. She was staying at a hostel right at the centre of downtown Toronto that had a very friendly vibe. She spent most of her days walking around and exploring King Street West, Queen Street, Chinatown, and Kensington Market. She was extremely happy to have explored and met up with her friends, but meeting Caio was the cherry on her sundae.

Caio came into the picture when they were dancing on the dance floor at a club downtown. He was tall, strong built, and had a prominent Portuguese accent. His typical Brazilian good looks were hiding under a grey newsboy hat, but he had that swagger that would catch your attention. He just grabbed her to dance and he was so sensual with his moves that one thing led to another, and they started kissing on the dance floor. She went with him to a dark corner of the club and made out like teenagers while Top 40 music was blasting in the background.

The night had to end with bright lights flashing in everyone's faces. She had to stay with her friend after the bouncers kicked everyone out of the club so she gave Caio her number and told him they could meet up the following evening, on her last night in Toronto. The next day, when her grade school friends were touring her around in a car, Caio was already text messaging her, wanting to make plans with her. She felt giddiness flowing through her after he told her to meet her at a bar called Spin, and gave her the address. There was something so exciting about meeting up with a good-looking guy in an unfamiliar place.

The next morning, she woke up in Caio's arms underneath his cozy comforter, feeling utterly satisfied, and right in that moment, she allowed herself to embrace all that warm and fuzzy feeling until she told him she had to go. He got her a cab, sent her off with passionate kisses and a promise to keep in touch as they said their goodbyes. He was incredibly sweet that it made her smile just thinking about it.

She shook herself up from her reverie and looked at her phone to check the time. The Broadway show was about to start. She tilted her face up to the sun one last time with her eyes closed and her lips curved up in a smile. This trip felt like such a gift, which she knew she deserved completely. She let the warm sunshine kiss her cheeks again, and felt this deep gratitude for everything. She stood up from the bench and started to walk up to the theatre, even more excited to watch the show.

When Love Hurts

When your love shines brightly it will only hurt when you hold on to it so tightly. Because when you love unconditionally, you don't need to possess; you give freely but it should always be a fine balance, no self-sacrifice but with self-love, no reliance. Learning to love yourself first, filling your cup, not giving in to lack and thirst. If you must love them from afar, you'll be fine, saying goodbye won't scar. You'll know you'll have a lot of love to give but also knowing how to fully receive. Love will only hurt when it is conditional, so when you let it go, you won't worry if it is not reciprocal. Because when you love yourself more, you won't keep score. Without losing yourself, you'll let the love exist, and you will soon enter a state of bliss.

To be Special

I didn't know what it was that made you truly special
Everything about you felt monumental
But that moment I stopped loving you was when I realized
That it was only my love that made you special in my eyes
Not the sparkle in your eyes or your charm
But my love for you that made me feel warm
And now that the love I wrapped you in disappeared
Your ordinariness began to appear

Confessions of a Former Addict

The truth is, I wouldn't let myself move on. Even when you stopped pulling on my heartstrings, I still searched for you. I was chasing those moments of pining over you like an addiction—toxic habit I couldn't shake off, because wanting you had become a part of me. You see, I had all these empty parts that were yearning to be filled. And you fit these parts like pieces of a puzzle, making me feel whole and complete. You made me feel this way just by me wanting you, until it finally stopped. Your pieces no longer fit the empty parts of me, because now they have been filled by me.

Gaze

The moment had passed
When you said goodbye
But your gaze stayed
With that look in your eye

The hope remained
Stabbed me in the heart
Tore me into pieces
Took me apart

Your gaze held hope
No words could ever say
Kept me stuck in a moment
Thoughts of you won't go away

But after years of heavy pining
With tearstained eyes
Your gaze faded over time
It was a pleasant surprise

Time still couldn't erase
Your gaze was like a tattoo
It is now dull and faded
But permanently marked by you

Love is Free

They said I had no reason to cry over you because those moments we had were brief and you were never mine. I tried to believe them only to realize that they were absolutely wrong. Love doesn't know time and ownership, because it's free.

Feel Anyway

They made me feel ashamed of my feelings for you
Created narratives that were not entirely true
Hushed whispers that I was hearing
Some betrayal that I was fearing
And all because of their twisted intention
My intuition I had to put into question
That even when I sat them down to ask
They never failed to put on these masks
Self-destruction had to take place
A round of applause for my fall from grace
But after many years of healing and introspection
I broke it down and saw the projection
They were ashamed of their own feelings
A fine distraction so they can continue concealing
Now that I know that my feelings hold power
I will always hold it in high regard and honour
I will never be ashamed of my feelings for you
Even if they consume me and make me cry over you

Perspective

When they rehashed the past many years later was the moment they both came to a realization. Each of them made their assumption about how the other felt about the connection, but ultimately, it was their own insecurity that affected their perspective, making their judgment defective.

Your Presence

Your greatest gift to me was your presence
No words, no gaze, just your lingering essence
I knew the moment would come when it wouldn't be enough
But I also knew that losing you would be tough
I hope one day your presence will grace someone special
And in her life you will become so essential
That she will love you for more than your presence
To continue to fight so she will never feel your absence

Passion

I already felt it right at that moment when I first saw you
Your big hazel eyes full of life
The red bandana on your forehead serving bad boy appeal
And I couldn't take my eyes off of you
Then we spent the rest of the night together
Wrapped in each other
Exploring the unexplored
Wanting more of one another
That each night of the week you spent it in my bed
And when you have left, you lingered
Parts of my body still tingling from your kisses
The scent of our passion all over the sheets

Not My Loss

I was so focused on the pain of not having you when I should have tried to understand your words more closely. You told me that I don't see myself the way you do, and that letting me go hurt you more than I would ever know. I grieved that loss so much, but now that I've healed and don't see it through the lens of heartache, I see it more clearly. You couldn't handle my shine; in hindsight, it was really your loss, not mine.

Muse

I could write a book about your gaze
A hundred poems to paint your face
But it could never be enough
Because putting you into words will be tough
You make my senses feel overloaded
Up and down but never jaded
You consume me in every way
I love and hate it, I must say
You're the one who inspires me to my core
That I keep on coming back for more
Because even if I completely refuse
I couldn't help that you're my muse

I Don't Remember You

She was tossing and turning in bed, feeling this strong pull to message him
It had been more than a decade since they last interacted
Her intention wasn't to tell him she was thinking of him or anything of that sort
But to clear away the cobwebs of the past
To clean up her side of the street
Leave things between them on a good note
She went over the message she was going to send him together with the story she'd written about the night that they'd met
Almost instinctively, she hesitated
She knew this was fear
Fear usually step[ed in when she did something out of her comfort zone
Then she immediately remembered that time when she reached out to another to tell him her deepest feelings
Now, that took courage and strength
Although she did it for herself
So she could feel lighter and free
His ice-cold response naturally made her feel bad
In this moment, she felt something had changed
She felt bolder, stronger, and wiser
As she was hitting send, she paused. *"What would be a horrible response to this message?* she asked herself
"Leave me on 'seen'?"
She chuckled to herself as she remembered those four words that she had previously received
And told herself, *"Anything, absolutely anything will be better than 'I don't remember you'"*
She chuckled once again and hit send

Holding Space

There's a room for you in my heart
Perhaps a little dusty and unkept
But on the walls I hung your favourite art
A space that I will always protect

Drama King

I slammed the door on your face many times before
But you keep on coming back for more
I have to say I admire your persistence
But you mask the reason for your insistence
All this drama that you create
It's even exhausting to enumerate
I see you sitting on your self-made throne
Crying over the affection I had once shown
Wearing that crown made of lies
And yet you wonder why you agonize
Don't you worry, you're still the king to be seen
But I'll never be your drama queen

Reflection

The moment you come to terms with the fact that the relationships you tend to keep mirror the relationship you have with yourself is the moment you start loving yourself more

The Morning After

She was really excited to see him last night and she knew that the feeling was mutual. They immediately gravitated towards one another the night that they met. It was an instant attraction. They kept in touch and hung out a couple times in bars with friends, but this was their first morning after. There was no doubt that they had chemistry and she definitely enjoyed their passionate rendezvous, but now that the excitement had worn off, she was feeling a little confused. As she sat beside him on the couch in the morning light, she was not feeling any kind of closeness towards him. They seemed to struggle to have a comfortable, effortless conversation. She was almost sure they had a connection, but as she thought about it more, alcohol and a group of friends were always involved when they were together. She looked at him again as he took a big gulp of coffee, feeling that physical attraction, but nothing else beyond that. That moment was when she realized: chemistry would get your foot in the door, but it wouldn't ever be enough for you to stay longer the morning after.

Soulmates

Maybe it was in another dimension
Perhaps a crack in space and time
Because I'm sure we were lovers
In a universe where I called you mine

The only reason you fit so perfectly
And how quickly we connected
How you affected me profoundly
That meeting you felt so fated

Perhaps this lifetime isn't ours
We were not meant to be together
But it didn't mean it was all a loss
You transformed my life beyond measure

Tag Heuer

I was having lunch with my sister when I was telling her about a guy I was seeing. She was carefully listening to my story when she asked me these questions — 1. What does he do for a living? 2. Where does he live? 3. What kind of car does he drive?... I paused to understand her questions and then told her with conviction that none of those things mattered to me. You see, before my fourteenth birthday, I was begging my dad for a Tag Heuer watch, thinking that wearing that watch on my wrist would make me so happy. I did get it as a birthday present, and I was initially so happy, but after a month, it lost its sparkle. One day, I was looking at its clock face on my wrist and placed it close to my ear to hear its soft ticking, still wondering where that happiness went. And in that moment, this watch, my fourteenth birthday present, taught me something very important about myself. It taught me that no material thing can ever give me that true happiness that lasts. So no, I'm not wanting someone who could buy me a Tag Heuer or any kind of luxury watch. I'm wanting someone who can make me forget the ticking of the clock, because time won't even exist in their presence.

Create Space

It wasn't enough for me to say goodbye. I had to let go of aspects of myself that were attached to you. I had to create space for new things in my life, and to allow for this new version of me to take place, so I could welcome new connections in this space.

Glow up

Your absence brought heartache
The heartache brought tears
The tears watered my garden
New growth appears

My flowers bloomed slowly
From all the tears that flowed
More seeds have sprouted
And from that growth, I glowed

You Were Not There

When I told you about the moment I had with that guy, you questioned it and filled my mind with doubt. But then, how could you know? You were not there. You were not part of that experience, so why would I let you shit on that moment that I hold so close to me? I don't know why you didn't want to believe me, but now I know that it doesn't matter. I realized that you probably will never know, because no one has ever looked at you the way that he looked at me.

My Power

I got it all wrong. I thought that when I'd given pieces of myself, I could never get them back. But it wasn't the case. The pieces of myself that I have given away hold power. Power that I was generously giving. Power in forms of thought, time, attention, care; and I could take them back, keeping them with me, holding on to them too, until I found someone truly deserving to give some of my power to.

Where it Lies

Her power lies in her vulnerability
Because it took courage to face her feelings
Her power lies in her honesty
Because it took strength to know her darkest parts
Her power lies in her boundaries
Because it took self-love to find her worth
Her power lies in her thoughts
Because it creates her reality
Her power lies in her feelings
Because it makes her human

And the moment she realizes where her power lies is when
the chaos in her connections subsides

Manifestation

It was the beginning of the school year when I found myself in your company. We were walking around the school campus after the final bell had rung. I was waiting for my ride to arrive when fate managed to orchestrate this moment with you. I didn't question what your intentions were and why you wanted to stick around on the empty school grounds with me. I just embraced the invitation like it was meant to happen. When you sat down beside me on the sidewalk, boredom and the potential frustration of watching the clock tick, suddenly became a sacred moment of wanting time to slow the fuck down. Those types of moments when you want to savour each second. I wasn't familiar with the term "manifestation" at this time. It wasn't a trendy buzz word in the 90's, but I was familiar with the feeling of "dreams coming true" in a Disney movie kind of way. I guess it was sort of a similar kind of energy, but a lot less grounded and more fantastical.

I'm not sure if you heard this through the grapevine but I was harbouring a massive crush on you for a few years before we finally met. I think I was 12 or maybe 13 when I saw you singing on stage in the school gym. I usually drift off during those boring school programs especially after lunch when the sun was at its peak, but your whole Eddie Vedder vibe kept me wide awake. I think it was known that the easiest and quickest way to my heart during that time was to embody Eddie Vedder. That scene, you on stage singing with your eyes closed and sounding like my favourite grunge god was etched in my brain. For a time, it had become a dreamscape I found myself escaping to.

I watched you closely but very discreetly since then. Lunch breaks became this quest of seeing a glimpse of you in the canteen. School suddenly became exciting. My ears were like radar; they searched for echoes of your name in school corridors and bathroom stalls. One sight of you and my day was made. A beautiful apparition in drab grey hallways. My notebook was filled with doodles of your name which I had to quickly erase. Other than the fact that you were a few years older than me, you were also not available. I sometimes saw you around school with your girlfriend and my ears rang whenever she spoke. Her voice sounded like fingernails on a chalkboard and I cringed every time. I often wondered what you saw in her and this thought came with enough self-awareness to know that it wasn't coming from jealousy. The girl who you decided to become your girlfriend was my older sister's best friend. Her voice was already screeching in my head even before the two of you became a couple.

My adoration for you was a steady trickle for two whole school years. Only a select few close friends from school knew this adoration firsthand. My neighbour and good friend who went to a different school was my safe space for all things related to you. One summer day, she excitedly told me that you were in the same summer school as her. She had to make up for the credits from failing some classes and you happened to be doing the same. She had this rushed energy when she came to talk to me because you, who apparently just became single, was eyeing her friend and schoolmate. My good friend had told her friend that I liked you for a very long time when she was talking about you and feeling all giddy about it. Her response to the statement of my adoration was - "all is fair in love and war".

That statement got my friend and I scheming. One day, when you were buying a drink at a nearby sari-sari store, my friend asked you nonchalantly if you knew my sister and I. She mentioned that we were neighbours and had grown up together. You answered "yes" to her without paying much attention but when she told you how much closer we were, your response was turning your head to her and saying "the sister?" with a big smile. She reported this news to me like I won the lotto which got us scheming even more.

The plan was for me to show up at the sari-sari store after your class with my friend. I was nervous, but those many years of adoration became a boost of motivation and you came up to me with the biggest smile on your face. When you asked me what I was doing there, I blurted my friend's name as an answer. You ignored my obvious anxiousness and continued talking to me. My anxiousness wasn't the only thing you ignored, you also ignored my friend's schoolmate which felt like a win.

But what felt more like a win was that moment with you in the empty school grounds. Your company, your attention, your full presence - it was a definite manifestation. When I saw both of our reflections on the school entrance glass door, something had hit me. It was when I realized how much I wanted and thought about this moment. Those times when I saw you walking around with your ex-girlfriend, I often wondered what it would be like to be doing the same with you. And after that moment, I don't have to ever wonder anymore.

The Idea of Love

I have always been in love with the idea of love. I will be ten steps ahead, and will create multiple stories in my head. When you show me the possibility of us, I will start imagining a future filled with love and lust. Because I'm a romantic at heart, and oftentimes it takes me apart. I will focus on your potential and everything about you that is special, but not so much on the reality, even your lack in reciprocity. Love will always be the end goal, what I thought I needed to make me feel whole. Until that moment when things have shifted, I realized my idea of love was twisted. Because love is cultivated within, and not something that I could win, so I stopped chasing, focused on myself, and continued embracing all the love for myself that I was craving.

Secret Thoughts

My secret thought is wanting you to manifest all of your secret thoughts of me. Because just by seeing the way you look at me, I already know that I want to experience all of your secret thoughts of me.

The Risk You Didn't Take

Heartbreaker, troublemaker
The ways that you described her
And yet you broke her heart
Caused her trouble when you chose to depart

Risk-taker, dream-maker
She would love you if you let her
She would take care of your heart
And she would accept your darkest part

To Forget

They were hugging tightly on the couch as sleep took over. In each other's arms, fully clothed, finding comfort in one another. When he had to go, he looked at her face, and he let his eyes linger. And when she said goodbye, she just knew why they spent the night together.

They had ghosts in their head that they both wanted to forget, and to have that moment of forgetting is a moment worth remembering.

Lesson

You were nothing but a lesson
A hard one to say the least
Even an unhealthy obsession
That was always meant to cease

You took me to the lowest of lows
Shot me down, killed my ego
Then received more series of blows
That came crashing like a torpedo

But the destruction was a disguise
The pain and heartache was a gift
Rebuilding myself was the prize
The lesson came with a major shift

It made me search for a better place
Created a stronger foundation
I bloomed faster with more grace
Allowed me to reach a new vibration

No Words Needed

We both fell silent
My mouth opened up
To say something
To break the silence
But I stopped
The silence was beautiful
And so comfortable
That we stayed there
In that moment
Where no words were needed

Yours to Carry

Those moments
spent with people
who refuse to take accountability
for their own shit
will make you realize
that their shit,
will also be yours to carry.

Unravel Me

I feel myself shattering under the sound of your voice
My heart pounding like I'll never ever have a choice
I easily come undone when I hear your name
That I bury my love for you with all of this shame
You make me feel out of control
Like you are the other part of my soul
I just don't know how you do it
How you make me go through it
I tried to fight it but I just have to let it be
To surrender and let you unravel me

Access

It felt like an ongoing uphill battle. She was sure she already knew her worth, but it felt like she was still on this neverending loop of disappointment. Until that moment she saw things more clearly. It wasn't enough to know her worth; she had to embody it and live it. She realized how accessible she had always been and people just took it for granted. But now that she knows what she has to do, she's only giving full access to a selected few.

Secret

You kept me like a dirty little secret
You hid me in an old attic, stuffed me in a dusty drawer
The moments we shared
To be long forgotten

I kept you like the most sacred secret
I put you in a gold locket, wore you on a chain close to my
chest
The moments we shared
Always to be remembered

Our secrets will be never the same
Even though they are one and the same

The Spark

She was looking out of their tour bus window, taking in all she could see of Berlin. She could still taste the alcohol in her mouth as she let the morning sunshine caress her face, giving her a boost of energy she desperately needed. She just had a conversation with her partner about the crazy, alcohol-fueled night that they previously enjoyed. They did a street art tour around Berlin, followed by bar-hopping with their fun-loving tour guides.

As they went over the events of the previous night, her partner mentioned how she instantly connected with one of their tour guides. He told her, "*you and the guy*", and motioned an explosion with his hands, without expressing any jealousy. She knew about this connection because she felt this to her core. It also seemed obvious to everyone around them. Her partner even walked away, looking annoyed that the tour guide left immediately after, most likely because of the tension he felt.

She did agree about the connection, but didn't say anything more. Nothing happened other than both of them simply conversing, which was hardly even flirting, but she also couldn't deny that spark. Her head was already pounding from being hungover, and to top that off, she was bombarding herself with so many thoughts and questions. She always believed that nothing was ever a coincidence. The fact that she was already neck-deep in thoughts and questions was already showing her that the spark that she felt that night was meant to ignite something within her. She was intently watching the fleeting sceneries of Berlin, but her mind was still hyper-focused on that brief moment of instant connection. And as the sceneries outside the window passed her by, she had this deep knowing that this spark was meant to affect her significantly, but how, she had yet to figure out.

The Driver Seat

You sat in the driver seat
Made me wait for you to come back
While you took many pit stops
Driving on this one-way track

With your hands on the wheel
Signaled where you wanted this to go
How long it will take to get there
Like it was only for me to know

Until it made me feel queasy
Who said you could be in control?
I had to pull the breaks
We're not driving to a one-man show

I finally got off this ride
But you didn't want to leave without me
You still sat in the driver seat
But would now take directions from me

Nothing to Do with Me

After making plans to meet up, he ghosted me. It made me feel insecure, wondering what it was about me that made him go away. After a short time, we reconnected and found out that his choice to disappear had nothing to do with me, but everything with him. He confessed his insecurities and was worried about how he would be received. He opened up about his wounds from the past, which put things into perspective. And all along, I thought I was not enough or even maybe I was too much, when the deeper truth is, it was him who was feeling not enough.

Magnet

I was drawn to you like a magnet
Kept searching for you all over this planet
A powerful pull I couldn't deny
The moment I saw that look in your eye

I tried so hard to run away
But I always got pulled back so I could say
The feelings for you that I've kept inside
With my true self that I also denied

And when I finally said my peace
My love for you stopped feeling like a disease
I no longer feel so immensely
You stopped pulling on me so intensely

You felt like a magnet to me
Because I had to make myself feel free
There was a deeper purpose for that pull
And it was to make myself feel whole

Closing Out a Cycle

Quite possibly the reason why we reconnected was to see how we projected, to close out a cycle, wrap our story up so it wouldn't be recycled. This was a way to shift our perspective, so we could finally change the narrative. Look closely at the roles that we played, and how they made us feel dismayed. A closure that would leave us at peace, it's a fine reason to say the least.

How to be With You

We shared a life for many years
Knew each other's dreams and fears
All the annoying habits and quirks
Found happiness when it works
Until we each took a different path
Accepted it wasn't meant to last
We met each other as a friend
Threaded carefully not to offend
Because it shouldn't be the same
How we used to call each other's name
But habits are hard to break
A new dynamic we need to make
Putting down boundaries when needed
So old ways won't be repeated
But we still don't know how to navigate
Blindly feeling it out to create
Until I had to put down some distance
And you showed some resistance
There was no other way to deal
But to let this connection heal
By completely saying goodbye for now
And hoping we can figure this out somehow
Because I don't know how to be with you
But I just know I can't be the same person you knew

A Dose of Me

It wasn't one size fits all. Different people, different reactions. Sometimes people get overwhelmed by how I make them feel. Needing only a few doses of me until they feel comfortable. Other people want dose after dose, needing more and more until I don't feel comfortable. But others couldn't handle any dose at all, and that is okay. You, not wanting a dose of me, reflects more on you than on me.

Dissonance

We couldn't see eye to eye
No matter how much I try
It isn't lack of communication
But more of comprehension
I shouldn't struggle to be understood
For you to know where I stood
Sometimes I feel so insulted
And to be honest, a little revolted
Because I shouldn't be always explaining
That I find myself complaining
It just means you truly don't know me
And you don't really see me for me

Ego Boost

We had been exchanging messages and photos for a while until we decided to meet up. You told me to meet you at a train station, so when I arrived, I was looking for the car you described. I saw you wave from the driver seat, but you drove past me, forcing me to walk across the street to meet you on the other side. When you stopped, I started to walk over. I felt your gaze watch my every move, but I didn't flinch. I walked slowly and ever so confidently towards you, and when I got to the passenger seat, the window was down and I said hello. If your eyes could pierce me, you could have cut me wide open. I opened the car door and slipped inside, tried gracefully to sit on the seat beside you, as you continued watching me with your mouth slightly open.

Out of Sight, Out of Mind

I remember looking out the window
And really feeling sad
The thought of not seeing you everyday
Made me a little mad

But today, I wasn't thinking of you
Not a single fantasy
I guess I just stopped liking you
A much better reality

Because we were both off-limits
We'll be going out of line
A relief that it happened organically
Out of sight, out of mind

Answers

I was endlessly searching for answers to understand
From the tarot deck in my hand
From the opinions that were said
From the signs that I've read
Yet the answers could only be given by you
And the answers I only want to hear are the ones that I know are true
Because deep inside I won't ever believe you
Even if you tell me, "*I don't feel the same way for you*"

The Art That is Love Bombing

I woke up with no messages from him and to be honest, it is making me feel weird. For more than a month now, I have been waking up every morning to his messages, so maybe I just got used to it. I mean, that should be the reason why I feel this way, right? I do enjoy our conversations but I think I'm sure that I'm not really into him. Today, though, when he didn't message me, it felt different, like I missed him somehow. Of course I'd be lying if I said that I don't enjoy the attention too because I do. Okay, so now I'm a bit confused, because I'm not sure why I'm not getting the same amount of attention anymore. Is it me? Did I say something? I'm actually thinking about this more and more. Oh my god. Am I starting to like him? I guess I'm going to have to be the one to message him again, which has been the case for the past few days now. Maybe I just really miss the attention. I don't know, but I'll just have to message him and see. I probably have to show more interest so he can give me back all the attention. Wait, I think I'm actually starting to like him...

Eskimo Kiss

Does true intimacy lie on the tip of the nose?
All my significant lovers did this the most
Rubbing their nose on my mine
Letting our feelings align
That I'll always feel true intimacy and bliss
When I receive an Eskimo kiss

Accountability

The moment when you refuse to be held accountable for how you made me feel is the moment I need to be held accountable for choosing you

How to Love Me

Peel back my layers
One by one
With swift precision
Slowly
Over time
Wanting more
Until you get to my core

Swim in my depths
With no fear
Or judgment
Only acceptance
Wrapping yourself in my essence

Climb up
To get to my greatest of heights
Not afraid to look down
Feeling it all out
Meeting me high above on the cloud

Appreciated

It had to take my absence to feel appreciated
All these years you took me for granted
Thinking that I could be easily replaced
Only now you are missing my embrace
It's unfortunate that you didn't see my value and worth
I'm too exhausted to try and make it work
I did tell you to make me feel special
So what you are facing is consequential
But thank you for telling me you appreciate me
I'm closing this chapter feeling more happy and free

The Deep Embrace

It was summer break when she ran away from home. She stayed with a friend for two weeks before moving to her best guy friend's house. She had been staying there for a week now. She slept in his room, on a rollaway bed that was kept underneath his bed whenever it was not in use. It felt so comforting to be sleeping close to him. They would watch TV at night before going to sleep just like an old married couple.

That night, after he turned off the light and he was laying down on his bed, he asked her if he remembered what he had told her at their friend's party many months ago. They were both drunk but she remembered it clearly. He confessed his feelings for her but she wasn't sure how she felt or how she should react to it even, so she laughed and pretended she didn't remember. She responded to his question with silence and he told her almost immediately after that he still felt the same way for her. They both welcomed the silence in the room, and then like an afterthought, he asked her for a hug. He often asked for hugs whenever they were together and that night felt like it was another one of those routine hugs. She climbed up to his bed and hugged him and right away, she knew that hug was different.

She wrapped her arms and her legs around him as he squeezed her tight. They felt each other's hearts beating through their chests. He was squeezing her even more tightly and then slowly and lovingly, he ran both his hands up and down her back. She felt so protected and cared for that she couldn't help but respond with the same amount of eagerness and warmth with her embrace. When he felt this, his body started to explore more, skin to skin, touch by touch, and she kept responding with equal passion. That was the moment they both surrendered to their feelings, embracing one another with all that they had. Until they heard a knock on the door, and they had to untangle themselves out of that deep embrace.

Ready to Lose You

I was waiting for you to give me more
But you showed no effort, my needs ignored
Poked you many times for a reaction
Still you continued to give me no action
Felt exhausted in the space that I was in
Realized that you had work to do within
And in that moment I decided to choose me
Cut all access, took back the key
Because I was finally ready to lose you
Than lose myself over an idea of you

The Bitter Pill She Swallowed

It was indeed the bitterness that tore her into pieces
Not because he chose somebody else
But because everyone had a say in it
It wasn't the moment when he chose to ditch her that stung
so bad
But the moment when she felt ganged up by his friends,
calling him up when they were with Each other, ordering
him to ditch her
It wasn't his rejection that hurt the most
But everyone's rejection of her happiness

Your Choices

I came to terms that it doesn't matter how you've felt for me or how much you've thought of me all this time. You still made that choice to go in another direction. All that should ever matter to me is the fact that you didn't choose me.

Meet Me There

It occurred to me in this moment of self-reflection
That what I wanted was a lot more than chemistry or compatibility or attraction
But your ability to meet me there
Your heart ready to open, your soul ready to bare
Show me how capable you are of learning and growing with me
Show me your accountability and your vulnerability
And perhaps we will be able to meet in this space of transcendent love
Not from codependence but a gift from above
Born out of our choice to completely evolve together
While fully supporting one another
And giving each other the freedom to be who we truly are
But closing the distance when we feel too far
If you could only meet me there
We could be with one another everywhere

Potential

That moment when her feelings finally stopped clouding
her judgment
Was when she finally saw the truth
He never broke her heart
She did that
He showed her many times who he truly was
Yet she insisted on loving him for the person that he could
be

My Hero

I was sixteen the first time I got completely wasted in public. Blame that cheap vodka, and of course my low tolerance to alcohol, which I hadn't quite figured out at that time. My friends and I went out to watch this band play. They mostly played classic rock and were starting to make waves in the local music scene with their original songs. The lead singer of the band was the good friend of the brother of one of my closest friends in high school. He was several years older than me and he had piercing eyes and long wavy light brown hair, which he usually kept in a ponytail. He looked every bit Hispanic, and with that voice and stage presence, he easily became a heartthrob.

He had always been nice, and I would say, a bit curious about me, but that night, he went out of his way to take care of me when I was drunkenly stumbling and going in and out of consciousness. He carried me all the way to the car, which he had to do more than once because I somehow managed to run back to the bar. I remember bits and pieces of that night, hanging on to him, having that feeling of being carried and whisked away. I looked up at him a few times when he was carrying me and during those moments when I was conscious, I watched the serious expression on his face with wonder. But one thing that will always stand out about that night was when I was sitting on a chair and he was crouched down and he asked, "*do you trust me?*" like he was the Aladdin to my Jasmine. And that was the moment when he became a hero to my sixteen-year-old self, and my drunken heart couldn't help but be completely and utterly smitten.

Honesty

Being honest with ourselves in relationships is so undervalued. We seem to always want an honest partner, always looking externally, but do we ever sit ourselves down and look inwards? Perhaps being honest with ourselves is what's needed to completely understand why things never seem to work out.

Read Between the Lines

I went over every word you told me, hoping to find hints of
love and care
Over over like your love would appear out of thin air
Riding this merry-go-round
Round and round, never getting off the ground
And I keep reading between the lines
Trying to find signs that will make your love align
Until clarity found its way to me
By letting things be, not wasting more of my energy
Because the only time I really should care
Is when you are certain, open-hearted, and willing to share

Grieve

She was walking outside, looking at the little droplets of rain touching the surface of the water in the lagoon. The chilly rainy fall day mirrored the feelings she had been harbouring inside. The cold air reflected the coldness she was feeling within. Even the falling leaves showed her the feeling of loss that had been consuming her. Even though she knew that this was what she wanted, her heart was still torn to pieces. It was difficult to say goodbye to a life that they built together, especially when that life wasn't bad. It wasn't emotionally fulfilling her, but it still had many beautiful moments.

She let the rain touch her face when her tears started to trickle down her cheeks, and this was the moment she knew. She was grieving. And in this space, she was deeply honouring her decade-long relationship, and the life that was built on that marriage.

Rebuilding

Experiencing loss will break you, but when you rebuild yourself, you will have a choice to make. Will you become hard or become soft? What direction will you take? Because it is all about lessons and how you will grow from your heartbreak.

Must Swoon at the Moon

Moments when the moon is so bright
You can see yourself glow from its silvery light
It's the most beautiful romantic sight
For myself, it's such a delight

But when I showed you the moon
You just shrugged, looked away so soon
That's when I knew we didn't sing the same tune
For my person must swoon at the moon

The Runner

I didn't run away from you, I ran away from myself. I ran away from my feelings just so I could protect myself.

The Chaser

I chased you because I needed your validation
To know that I'm deserving of your time and affection
I chased you so you could show me that I'm worthy
To know that I'm lovable so I could be happy

Comfort Zone

You chose safety over untamedness
You chose preservation over vulnerability
You chose convention over passion
Needing this stable ground
Until that moment when your run-of-the-mill choices had
left you hungry, wanting more
Standing on this unstable ground
Feeling that feeling you tried to avoid all along
Now fully understanding that fulfillment only blossoms
outside of your comfort zone

Overgiver

I can't put all the blame on you
When I always overgive
I wanted you to give the same to me
No choice but to forgive
Because at the end of the day
I really should have known
The moment to stop to give
When reciprocity was not shown

Running on Empty

She just gave without you asking
And you took from her
Even demanding, wanting more
Not bothering to fill her up
Or even checking if she had anything more to give
It had to come to this moment of exhaustion
For her to finally stop
And to start giving to herself
Slowly filling herself up
Of everything she had ever given you

Grey Area

I stay in these grey areas
Because the moment I look at things in black and white
Is when hope between us fades away

Everywhere

I am trying so hard to forget you, but the universe doesn't want me to. I see your name everywhere, on car plates, store signs; I turn around, and it is there. And that wasn't enough, seeing your face makes it more tough. I turn on the TV and there you are. Your face on Coca-Cola posters I see near and far. I flip through a magazine, and I can't catch a break. I see your face smiling, I whisper, "*for fuck's sake*".

You are just everywhere, also in love songs and in the air. You creep up the moment I wake up, and you cling on to me when I get up. So don't blame me if I can't forget you, when there is no way I could escape you. You know, you follow me everywhere; even in my dreams you are always there.

Always Mine

I wouldn't share my sadness with anyone
Because they told me that he was never mine
But I cried anyway
Underneath my blanket where no one could see me
The tears flowed endlessly
And in this moment I just knew
That even if he was never mine
The sadness that I had felt
That will always be mine

The Space Between Us

When the space between us
Feels heavy and loud
It's time to close the distance

When the space between us
Feels peaceful and calm
It's time to keep the distance

The space between us will know
If there are still moments to share
And if the connection can grow

The space between us can tell
If it will be worth it to stay
Or to finally bid farewell

Wedding Ring

My marriage sat comfortably in my life just like the wedding ring on my finger. The moment I took it off, I felt its absence linger. A security blanket that kept me safe and stable, then became a question about if I was still good enough and able. To feel free and to start fresh, and to say goodbye to things that no longer meshed. It would take a little getting used to, but now I had a chance for a breakthrough. The moment that I placed my wedding ring in my drawer, I completely opened that door to this whole new chapter, where choosing me was a major factor.

The Risk

Take the risk of not knowing
Or the risk of your heart breaking
It will always be a gamble
If you'll stand straight or stumble

What risk would you take
For moments you could make
You could let her take you apart
Or you could always break your own heart

Lovesickness

I called out your name when his fingers were inside me,
and in that moment of pleasure, I felt even more empty.

The Boys of Summer

It was summer of 2021, the summer she turned forty-three. She officially moved out and separated from her husband of nine years. She was moving back to Manila in the fall and had been unemployed for several months. Fortunately, she was collecting employment insurance from the government, which gave her the financial support that she needed so she could hang back and enjoy summer in Vancouver. Being newly single, she wanted to get out there and date, celebrate her freedom and have fun. She was not looking for anything more than that since she was leaving the country. She was a little bit worried about getting out there because she got married before dating apps changed the dating world. She knew she would have to figure out how to navigate the new ways. Also, she was in her forties; she didn't know how marketable she was at that age, but after chatting and exchanging photos for some time, she did get more confident. She had a bunch of exchanges and met up with several of them. Even though it was frustrating sometimes, she was having a great time. She had been learning a lot about men as well, and the pressure they put on themselves to show up a certain way. More importantly, she was significantly growing through her interactions. She watched herself put down boundaries and communicate what she wanted a lot more openly. It has been such a ride that she could very much say that the summer of 2021 was one for the books.

That night she was meeting Jack. They didn't exchange much but she was somehow intrigued by him. He told her he didn't want to send her a photo but he claimed that he was gorgeous and she would have to take his word for it. There was something about the way he delivered it that made her open to seeing him. They made plans to meet before sundown at the boardwalk by the Fraser river, so there she was, scanning the area. She was looking for someone who looked like he was looking for someone, because all he told her was that she would just know it was him.

She immediately saw a man with dirty blonde hair leaning on the railing of the boardwalk, almost posing like a model. He was wearing a button-down shirt with floral print and white Native sneakers, which was the same footwear that she was wearing. He was very good-looking, she had to admit that, but she still would not call him gorgeous. He turned and looked at her, gave her a charming smile, and started to walk over.

Denial

The moment I saw her hand in yours
Was when I realized
That I always wanted to be yours
And I was not surprised
I guess I have been in denial
Of what I was feeling for you
Maybe it was a way of survival
So I couldn't feel more for you

My Heart and Everyone

My beating heart
Searched for love that was true
Needed your kiss
Looked in everyone for you

My broken heart
Had tears like rain
Flooded my town
Drowned everyone with pain

My healed heart
Was like the summer sun
Shined so brightly
Gave warmth to everyone

Never Mine

You told me that I had you
I didn't know what you meant
You belonged to another
Did this mean you were not content?

I couldn't claim you
Was all that I knew
I couldn't hug and kiss you
And that felt like a blow

So even if you said that I had you
It would never be enough
I knew she would say, "*he's mine*"
And I could never call her bluff

Never Hers

For years she calls you hers
While your mind swirls and stirs
Filling you with thoughts of another
Making you a distracted partner

But you find comfort in settling
Make it work, stop battling
And she keeps up with the show
Because her intuition will always know

The Pull

I can attest that when I feel a pull towards someone, there is a deeper purpose for it. If it's not love or relationship that will blossom, I know for a fact that it will be a lesson.

Codependency

I questioned whether you loved me truly
Or you really just needed me
But then again if I had to question
There must have been some sort of confession
Because there was this sense of deficiency
That created this codependency
And this wasn't the love that I wanted
That these thoughts kept my mind haunted
I got lost in deep introspection
Then came to a realization
My love for you also came from a place of need
Holding on would slowly make my heart bleed

He was there

I could let your lack of attention affect me, but he was there. The look he just gave me just made up for your silence and the attention you have given others. His mere presence just made me forget your existence for a delicious minute or two. And I thank the universe for letting him walk into my life, because he always reminds me something about myself that I keep on forgetting with you around. He reminds me of how attractive I am and how deserving I am of the attention that you refuse to give me.

The Shift

One day she woke up
Felt differently
Questioned how you showed up
Saw everything clearly

And that was the moment
When the game had changed
An internal movement
Where hearts would be rearranged

Intimacy

It wasn't that first time when we took our clothes off that I felt intimate with you. It was that time you asked me why I didn't have a good relationship with my mom. That made me feel more naked and vulnerable, but at the same time, safe.

Intuition

She received a message from him asking her to come over. She thought why not, she could use a lover. But as she was walking to his place, she suddenly slowed down her pace. She went over their conversation; there was something off with his flirtation. She called her friend to help her figure it out and decided she should just back out. She messaged him and explained her hesitation, and he responded with so much passive aggression. In this moment she knew exactly why she felt the need to forget about this guy.

When we listen carefully to the whispers and subtlety, we will eventually hear it loudly. It is our intuition giving us clear direction, simply for our protection.

In Dreams

Meet me again in dreams
Where we are always free
Do the things we want to do
A safe place for you and me

Polarity

How can a brief moment of pure bliss and pleasure easily turn to a long lingering moment of yearning and pain?

Our Bubble

It felt like it was just you and me in this world
Maybe we were in another dimension
Encapsulated in euphoric bliss
A place beyond comprehension
And when they tried to get inside
They weren't able to come through
This bubble that cocooned us both
Was only for me and you

The Importance of Self-Love

It's funny how you keep insisting on the narrative that you want to run with. The illusion that you want to hold on to because it makes you feel better about yourself. Clearly, your own misery is needing some company, and it decided to zero in on me. You actually thought that I'd believe your malicious bluff when there were tell-tale signs of your psychological projection. And when I debunked the bullshit that you'd been throwing at me, your irrational anger erupted violently. That was the moment you completely gave yourself away. Your wretchedness and self-loathing were so deep-seated that my infuriation quickly transformed to empathy . Not only did I feel sorry for you, I also could imagine what it would be like to look at yourself in the mirror and hate what you saw. Yes, you can continue with your self-deception, but know that it won't stop all those people you claim don't like me to stop adoring me. Most importantly, it won't change the image that you see in the mirror or the feelings you have about yourself. You will only loathe yourself more, because I will continue to shine and you will soon find out that no matter how hard you try and cry about it, you can't ever dim my light. Why? Because unlike you, I have faced and embraced all of my darkest parts, and the beautiful end result of this process is self-love. Because the reality of it ultimately is—how we treat others is how we treat ourselves.

Stories

We sat down and told our stories
Shared our many dreams and worries
Showed each other our trophies and scars
Under the light of the moon and the stars

We shared moments, created stories
Made each other our sacred territories
We hugged, cried, and stayed together
Until time told us we were done and over

We said goodbye, took our stories
In our solitude, we did inventories
Put all the best ones on our shelf
With the old versions of our self

Rejection

It took some time to fully understand it
My heart had to break and had to mend it
It wasn't that you didn't want to be with me
But you knowing the capacity to be hurt by me

Chemistry

One day, someone will walk into your life and give you the attention you didn't know you needed, and you will no longer be the same. You don't know what it is about them that makes you want to see them again and again. Just a glimpse, and your day is made. Is it the way they walk? The way the soft waves of their hair crown their head? The way their lopsided smile adds a distinctive charm to their face? It's hard to decide what it is about them that makes you want to see them, because you just don't know. You swear they are not your type, yet you feel giddy when they give you hints of mutual attraction. You even make promises to yourself to stop looking, but when you see them, you just can't help yourself. You have a knee-jerk reaction to their presence. And then, you finally stopped asking and you start basking in that feeling. Because that was the moment when you came to terms with the fact that chemistry refuses to be understood or defined.

Catfished

You seemed so paranoid about me not being the person I said I was, but when I met you at that place, the photo you sent looked nothing like your face. You played a stupid game so you won a stupid prize, and that was me slamming the car door, much to your surprise.

Pedestal

I built you a pedestal
Made with pure gold and honey
The way it gleamed and glimmered
Could make any grey day sunny

I put you on that pedestal
Made you a beautiful shrine
Brought you candles and flowers
You should have seen yourself shine

But the flowers withered and died
Candles burned out with your name
The pedestal fell apart with my heart
When you said, *"the feeling is not the same"*

Romanticism

If I could only write
Our moments together
That I created in my head
We'd have the greatest
Love story ever to be read

My Favourite Candy

I've never tasted anything so exquisite in my life. I want it to stay in my mouth so I can suck on it forever. And I will never stop wondering how anything could taste and feel so sweet. Your tongue will always be my favourite candy.

I Regret You

I regret meeting you
At that time when I was feeling brand new
It was how we connected so easily
Conversations flowed too freely
And how we were strikingly similar
That you felt incredibly familiar
Even the people around us could see
That bright spark between you and me
You had a presence that persisted
And touch that I never resisted
You opened that door to our potential
Made me feel so fucking special
And then you just took it away
So quickly to my dismay
That brief moment lingered the longest
The feeling I felt was the strongest
I regret that time we spent together
Because I wanted to live in that moment forever
And even if you said you couldn't stay with me
Since that moment I was never free

One Chance

I was pouring tea for my aunt when I heard your voice. Your presence immediately called my attention. You sat across from me at the table right next to us, possibly dining with your mom. My eyes were grazing your well-defined features as you read the menu. I'm sure you felt my gaze because you looked up and quickly made eye contact with me. When you ordered your meal, your voice sounded clear and crisp, making my ears perk up. Even more so when I was trying to figure out the language you were speaking when you conversed with your companion. I felt your presence becoming stronger and I couldn't resist looking at you from time to time, only to find out that I wasn't the only one sneaking glances in between bites of food. We had moments when we both looked at each other a little longer, and for some reason, that didn't feel awkward. When we had to go, I felt you watching me as I stood up from the table, and when I was waiting outside for my companions, I watched you when you started to leave. You, with your skateboard in hand, came close to me and smiled, and I just stood there looking at you blankly. When you turned and walked away, I watched you from behind and I told myself, *"you had one chance, ONE CHANCE"* and just like that, you were gone.

Gas Works Park

Supposedly a great day with you
Green grass and warm sunshine
But I cried over the best city view
Unshed tears built up with time

I had to walk away from you
My broken heart in my hand
With all the frustrations that grew
Even if I tried to understand

You could never make me feel
Like that bright shining star in your life
You did bring up my wounds to heal
But you still cut me like a knife

So right at that moment, in that place
A decision had been made
Gas Works Park made me embrace
It's where my value had been laid

Paper Cuts

And I thought I should learn how to not let it affect me. The way you leave me on "seen" and then leave your digital footprints elsewhere. But it turns out that there is a deep cut that I am not fully aware of. Something you'd done way back then that cut me. It scabbed over time because of distance from you, but that cut was never healed because it was not acknowledged. It had a chance to when we reconnected, and you apologized for it, but you kept doing what you'd done to me again and again on a smaller scale. I didn't consciously know it, but you have been giving me tiny little cuts like annoying paper cuts whenever you ignore me until that old cut reopened. And that cut started oozing fresh blood and was only getting deeper with every tiny cut that you give me; you can say that they mean nothing, but to me, apparently they mean everything. You see, that cut started to run deep, and if I don't make it stop, it will slowly affect how I see and feel about myself. Because you make me feel like I'm not worth your time, effort, and attention. And if I believe that, I will be that. And I know it isn't true. Because how you decide to treat me doesn't have anything to do with me or my worth. But now it is up to you because I won't let you cut me anymore. I will only allow you back if you lick my cuts clean and acknowledge that even the tiniest paper cut can hurt.

Feel Deeply

To all fellow sensitive souls
To those who could never fit any role
Allow yourself to feel deeply
Never be ashamed to love completely
Let your whole being feel
Even if you have to surrender and kneel
Because to feel deeply is a gift
Just let your emotions drift
Learn to ride the ebbs and flows
And one day you will know
That being human is to truly feel
Making our experiences so beautifully real

Prerequisite

After more than a year of confusion and not seeing each other, we still found ourselves on the couch, silently cuddling, feeling at peace with one another. And that moment of hushed contentment was when I made a promise to myself. Cuddling in silence will now be a prerequisite.

Connection

A deep conversation
Your forehead touching mine
Sensing your vibration
Losing track of time

Being fully present
No struggle to be understood
Safety in your presence
An interest in my childhood

Looking deep in your eyes
Laughing at each other
All these feelings arise
Wanting more of one another

Never Easy

If it was as easy as one-two-three, we'd already know what this thing is between you and me. But so many things are in the way, or maybe that's just what you say. Because all these things that make it tough just make me feel like I'm not enough. But I know that you feel it, though, so why do we still not know? How we can make "us" happen, act on our feelings and feel so golden. Perhaps it's true what they say, that nothing worth having will easily come our way. But god, it's so frustrating, when you feel like you're in limbo and you don't want to be waiting. Then I finally let go. Didn't shut the door, but will focus on myself and grow. Maybe I'll meet you on the other side, when we both feel like we've got nothing to hide. And then we'll know for sure, even with all the grievances and the detour. That it will be worth it in the end, proving that our love will transcend. And if I don't meet you there, you still taught me healthy love and care. Because self-love was never easy to attain, but because of you, I learned and feel this in my veins. You see, I win either way; it was never easy, but I'll have the biggest takeaway.

That Look

It was that moment when you walked right in front of me, and you shot me that look. I don't know if you planned it, or if it was purely instinctive, because I found myself looking right back at you. And we just knew. The attraction was strong and mutual. And if all we could do to act on the attraction was to look at each other longingly, I'd take it. The look you'd given me meant so much more than some of the kisses I've received and have given. That look needed no words, because describing it is restraining it. And I don't want to do that. We already need to restrain ourselves from each other, so I will let that look do its magic. To fill me, inspire me, and to love deeply.

Excuses

I made excuses for you
Controlled the narrative to keep on seeing you
Made it seem that I won't be in the losing end
Even when you make me feel so drained and spent

I repeated the excuses I made for you
Hoping one day we would see this through
Always justifying why you never showed up for me
The way you kept silent and let the clock tick on me

I stopped making excuses for you
Because one day I woke up and saw my heart anew
The excuses were made to hold on to the idea of you
But the reality of you never deserved the excuses I made
for you

Boomerang

I did feel bad when you told me that you don't remember me after I had told you that I had unconditional feelings for you, but that feeling didn't linger. Not only did I get my closure and bury you, I was also told a few years after that I had been in someone's thoughts for more than a decade. Like you, I now know how it feels to be pleasantly surprised in that way. That moment solidified my belief in the universal law of karma, because that love that I put out had found its way back to me in another form. A beautiful boomerang that I have acknowledged and have gratefully received.

Hearts Everywhere

I swore I lost my heart
I looked for it on my lover's bed until it fell apart
I searched for it in my new friend's eyes
Even tried to win it like a prize
I carefully listened to the whispers in the air
Because maybe I could find it there
I dug around in everyone's chests to see
Perhaps my heart was left there for me
Then I stopped looking around, looked within
And realized it was where it had always been
Yes, my heart was there all along
And when I found it, I knew I was wrong
My heart was never lost
It was slowly ripped apart and tossed
I was chasing my broken heart's ghost
Because that pain was what I needed to heal the most
So I sat down with the pain, let my heart cry
And now that it healed, I don't even need to try
I don't only see my heart beating there
I also see hearts everywhere

As Within So Without

That moment when you realize that his choices had
nothing to do with how much he likes you, but everything
about how much likes himself, is the moment you stopped
questioning your worth.

Heart > Ego

On days like this when I'm feeling an emotional low and feeling that strong desire to be with someone, I question my choices. Why can't I be just like those people who seem happy with choosing a partner for egotistical reasons? At least they're not alone. At this moment, I envy them. I envy their contentment for their choices and the lasting fulfillment that it brings them. It truly isn't easy sometimes to know your heart's desire and hold out for it even if it isn't materializing. But after I feel all the feelings and move through that heaviness, I come back to my senses. I know that kind of happiness won't last for me, so why even go there? I know this because I have settled once before. Although I can say that it was what I needed and wanted at that time, it had served its purpose. And now, my heart is screaming even more loudly. It's telling me to stand my ground because there is a reason for this desire. There is just a deep knowledge that the universe won't let me long for something that I cannot have. So, I tell my ego to be still and be patient, because one day, the heart will win it all and it will be everything that I've ever wanted and more.

Ghost

A ghost with many faces comes to visit me whenever I'm brokenhearted and sad. It lurks in the shadows, ready to pounce like a predator wanting its prey. But last night, when it came, I asked, "*Why do you come to visit me?*" and it replied, "*Your broken heart asked me to*", and that was the moment I knew what I had to do. I have to thank my ghost because it is showing me what I need to heal the most.

Library of Moments

Collect moments, not things
Write stories the heart brings
Connect deeply with another
Make a moment last forever